A field guide to
Summer

To the wonderful pupils of Griffin Primary, an inner-city school that has planted a tree for every child. And to their former teacher Louise Black, whose reading of the poem "Meadow Flowers" inspired this whole series of books!—G.D.

For Antoni, Hannah, and Emmelie. May you find joy in every season.—D.B.

A Field Guide to Summer © 2025 Thames & Hudson Ltd, London
Text © 2025 Gabby Dawnay
Illustrations © 2025 Dorien Brouwers
Forest School consultant: Louise Black

All Rights Reserved. No part of this publication may be reproduced or transmitted in any form or by any means, electronic or mechanical, including photocopy, recording, or any other information storage and retrieval system, without prior permission in writing from the publisher.

First published in the United States of America in 2025 by
Thames & Hudson Inc., 500 Fifth Avenue, New York, New York 10110

Library of Congress Control Number 2024935645

ISBN 978-0-50065-353-1

Impression 01

Printed and bound in China by
Toppan Leefung Printing Limited

MIX
Paper | Supporting responsible forestry
FSC® C104723

Be the first to know about our new releases, exclusive content, and author events by visiting
thamesandhudson.com
thamesandhudsonusa.com
thamesandhudson.com.au

A field guide to Summer

Gabby Dawnay
Illustrated by Dorien Brouwers

what's inside?

6	**Wild by nature** Welcome to summer	22	**We're going on a bug hunt!** Searching for creepy-crawlies
8	**Sensing summer** Noticing nature's changes	24	**Hungry caterpillars** The life cycle of a butterfly
10	**Meadow flowers** A poem to read in a field	26	**Fluttering butterflies** Why butterflies love flowers
12	**Bright and beautiful** Summer flowers in full bloom	28	**Summer wings** Make a hapa zome butterfly
14	**Petal power** How to identify wildflowers	30	**Marvelous moths** What do you know about moths?
16	**A crown for summer** Make your own flower crown	32	**Summer sing-along** A poem to read at sunrise
18	**Busy, busy bees . . .** What honeybees do all day	34	**Wake up!** Listen to the dawn chorus
20	**Buzzing and bumbling** How to identify bees		

36	**Under shady branches** Spending time with trees	50	**Keeping cool** How to be cool when it's hot
38	**Tree ID** How to identify trees by their leaves	52	**Treasure hunt** Searching for signs of summer
40	**Lumps and bumps** Make your own bark rubbings	54	**A lazy summer day** A poem to read in the shade
42	**Sunny days** And warm nights	56	**Be prepared** Tips for the outdoors
44	**Keeping time** Make your own sundial	58	**Field notes** Recording summer's changes
46	**Free your feet** Going barefoot outdoors	60	**Summer words**
48	**Cloud gazing** What can you spy in the sky?	62	**Index**
		64	**About the author and illustrator**

wild by nature

Welcome to summer

Let's learn all about summer by spending time in the wild. Because the more you spend time with nature, the better friends you'll become.

You will find that by being CURIOUS about nature, CREATIVE in nature, and KIND to nature you'll quickly become a nature expert. There's so much fun to be had just by playing, talking, asking questions, and getting creative in the wild. So what are you waiting for?

HOW TO MAKE NATURE YOUR FRIEND

BE CURIOUS
What questions spring to mind?
What do you know?
What don't you know?
How can you find out more?

BE CREATIVE
Take the time to look closely at nature.
What colors, shapes, and patterns do you notice?
What connections can you find?

BE KIND
Imagine the world from a bug's point of view . . .
. . . or from a bird's.
How old is this tree and what has it seen?
If you were a flower, would you want to be picked?

📖
LEARN
Discover more about nature.

♡
FEEL
How do you feel in nature?

☆
BE
Be a part of nature.

sensing summer

Noticing nature's changes

The colorful signs of summer have arrived! There are bright flowers with sweet perfumes, busy insects, and leaves flourishing in every shade of green.

> Go for a walk and find a tree that is away from noisy roads and playgrounds. Stand with your back to it.
>
>
> **SMELL** — Close your eyes and take a deep breath. What can you smell?
>
>
> **LISTEN** — Stand very still and listen to the sounds. What can you hear?
>
>
> **LOOK** — Open your eyes slowly, as if you've just woken up. What can you see?
>
>
> **TOUCH** — Crouch down and touch the ground. What can you feel?
>
>
> **TASTE** — Stretch up to the sky and lick your lips. What can you taste?

Whether you live in a busy city or quiet countryside, you can use your super senses to spot the changes in nature as they happen. Have you noticed any of these signs lately?

THE SIGNS OF SUMMER

LEAVES are lush and green

HOT WEATHER, more sun, and less rain

LONGEST DAYS and shortest nights

BUTTERFLIES flutter in the sunshine

BIRDS singing loud and clear

SWEET SCENTS of flowers fill the air

GRASS grows long

BUSY INSECTS buzz, hum, and chirp

BLUE SKIES are full of fluffy clouds

meadow
flowers

A poem to read in a field

Fluffy-puffy
Seeds rise . . .
Dancing fairies in disguise!

Flying up
Bobbing low
Little seeds where will you go?

Over meadows
Full of flowers
Sun and rain, wind and showers . . .

Through the woods
Over trees
Carried high upon the breeze . . .

Flying up
Dip and drop
Little seeds where will you stop?

Grasses sway
Grasses grow
Flowers come and flowers go . . .

Flying bees
Insects flutter
Butterflies on cups of butter!

Daisy, daisy
Love me do
Golden corn and flowers blue . . .

Poppy patterns
Dotting red
Through a multicolored spread!

Yellow lions
In the sun
Dandelions for everyone!

Where there are flowers, there are bees. Can you hear them buzz?

bright and beautiful

Summer flowers in full bloom

Dazzling MARIGOLDS and GERANIUMS send insects into dizzy spins of delight. ASTERS, PEONIES, RHODODENDRONS, and HYDRANGEAS bloom in a flower rainbow across parks and gardens.

Tiny purple flowers appear on perfumed LAVENDER, while ROSES and HONEYSUCKLE unfurl scented petals. Warm air carries their fragrances further, attracting insects like bees and butterflies.

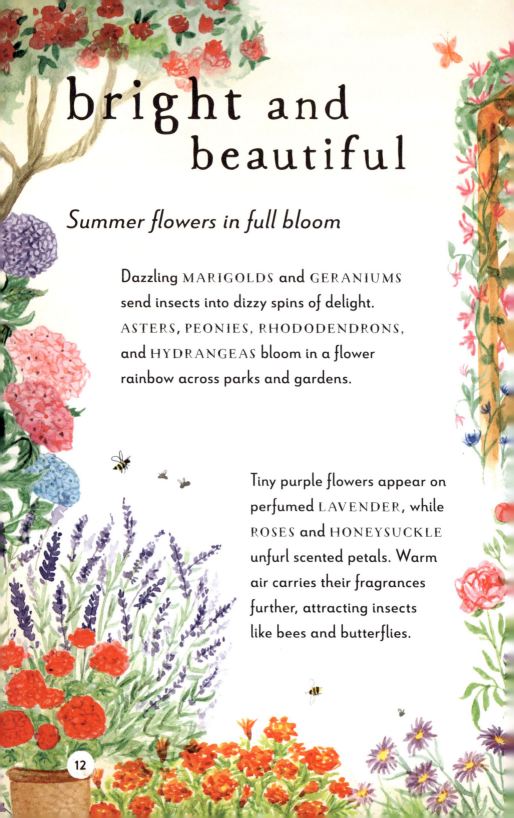

👃 SMELL Which flowers have the strongest scent?
👄 TASTE Some flowers, like honeysuckle, make sweet, edible nectar.

Meadow flowers bask in the warm sunshine. Great fields of green become peppered with paper-petaled POPPIES and spiky, blue CORNFLOWERS.

SUNFLOWERS turn their glowing faces upward toward the sun, each yellow head following its path across the sky.

Golden DANDELIONS turn into fluffy white globes. A gentle breeze or puff of breath sends fairy umbrella seeds dancing!

petal power

How to identify wildflowers

POPPY
- Bright red flower
- Large, round petal
- Black center
- Prickly stem

BUTTERCUP
- Bright yellow flower
- Five cup-shaped petals
- Branching stem

👁 SEARCH for meadow flowers in towns and gardens, as well as fields and grasslands.

CORNFLOWER
- Bright blue flower
- Dark purple center
- Long, pointy leaf
- Upright stem

What color is the flower?
What shape is the petal?
What shape is the leaf?

DANDELION
- Golden yellow flower
- Narrow, rectangular petal
- Jagged-edged leaf
- Bendy stem

A dandelion's golden petals are quickly replaced by fluffy seed heads.

a crown for summer

Make your own flower crown

Dress yourself in summer by making a flower crown. They are fun to make outside and would be a lovely gift for a friend!

PROTECT PLANTS

- Some flowers are rare and precious, so you should always ask an adult before picking anything.

- Daisies, dandelions, and buttercups are perfect for making crowns, and you can find lots of them all over the place!

- Never pull a plant up from the root. Snip or break off the stem instead.

1. Pick a handful of flowers with long stems (ideally at least the length of your thumb.) Remove the leaves, if there are any.

2. Take one flower and use your fingernail to make a little slit toward the end of the stem.

3. Thread the stem of another flower through the slit.

4. Make another slit in the stem of the second flower.

5. Thread a third flower through that slit and continue this process until you have a chain long enough to wrap around your head.

6. To form your crown, make a slightly bigger slit in your final stem and gently push the head of your first flower through it.

TIP *Why stop with a crown? You can make bracelets and necklaces the same way!*

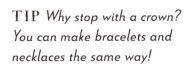

busy, busy bees . . .

What honeybees do all day

Bees are **pollinating insects**. This means that they perform the important job of carrying **pollen** from flower to flower. Most plants need pollen from other flowers to make seeds. So bees are essential for plants to flourish.

HONEYBEES live together in hives. A group of honeybees is called a colony and its members include the queen, thousands of female worker bees, and hundreds of male drones.

In summer, the drones protect the hive while the worker bees fly out to collect pollen and **nectar** from flowers. Pollen and nectar are bee food.

👄 **TASTE** Next time you have a spoonful of honey, just imagine the bees that worked so hard to make it!

📖 **LEARN** Honeybees do a special "waggle dance" to give other bees directions to good flower patches.

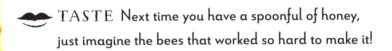

Bees collect pollen in tiny pouches on their legs to bring back to the hive. But little bits of pollen fall off their fuzzy bodies, pollinating plants as they travel to and fro.

Honeybees use their precious nectar to make honey for the colony. Honey is the only insect-made food that humans can eat.

buzzing and bumbling

How to identify bees

There are more than 20,000 different types of bee in the world! Honeybees and bumblebees are **social bees**, which means they live together in colonies, but most bees are **solitary bees**, which means they live alone. Each female makes her own nest, but they often live close together.

American bumblebee

Red-tailed bumblebee

BUMBLEBEES
- Round, fluffy body
- Different colors depending on type
- About 0.4 to 0.9 inches long

Wool carder bee

LEARN Wasps are closely related to bees. It's right to be careful around wasps as they might sting you if upset them. But they are important pollinating insects and deserve our respect, just like bees!

Wasp

HONEYBEES
- Slim body
- Black and gold stripes
- About 0.4 to 0.6 inches long
- Live in hives

Honeybee

Leafcutter bee   *Miner bee*

Ivy bee

SOLITARY BEES
- There are over 3,000 types of solitary bee in the US alone.
- They vary in size, shape, and color.
- Some are fluffy, like bumblebees, but others are almost completely hairless.

we're going on a bug hunt!

Searching for creepy-crawlies

Bug hunting is so much fun, and a fantastic chance to discover wildlife all around you! You don't need any special equipment, but you might want a notebook to record what you find.

WHERE TO LOOK

Bugs live in lots of different places, from shady woods to sunny meadows, garden beds to pavement cracks.

Millipede

Grasshopper

- Peep under logs and rocks.
- Look closely at leaves and flowers.
- Search among tall grass.
- Get down low to the ground.
- Check in the cracks of trees.

Ladybug

Pill bug

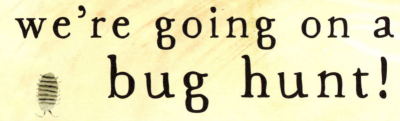

Snail

 LOOK Watch how they move. What are they doing?

Once you've found a creepy-crawly, a great way to get to know them is to leave them be and watch them in their natural surroundings. If you have a magnifying glass, use it to take a closer look without disturbing them.

STAG BEETLE ALERT!

If you spot one of these rare beetles you are very lucky! Male stag beetles have big jaws that look like antlers, but a female's jaws are much smaller.

Centipede

Ant

Male stag beetle

Slug

hungry caterpillars

The life cycle of a butterfly

When a butterfly is born, it has a completely different body from the body it has as an adult. Follow the phases of the butterfly's **life cycle** to discover how this wonderful transformation takes place.

1. A monarch butterfly starts life as a tiny egg. The egg is laid on the leaf of a milkweed plant by a female butterfly.

 LEARN In total, the journey from egg to butterfly takes around 24 days.

2. Out of the egg hatches a caterpillar. The caterpillar grows from the size of a pinhead to 2 inches long within the space of two weeks.

How does a caterpillar grow so fast? By eating enormous amounts of food!

3. The caterpillar attaches its back legs to the stem of the plant. It wraps itself inside a protective casing called a **chrysalis**. Inside the chrysalis, the caterpillar transforms into a butterfly. This process is called **metamorphosis**.

4. The monarch butterfly takes 10 days to transform from a chrysalis to an adult butterfly. The chrysalis splits open and the butterfly prepares its wings to start flying.

fluttering butterflies

Why butterflies love flowers

Have you ever followed a butterfly around a park or a garden, or through a forest? Where does it like to land? Just like bees, butterflies fly from flower to flower in search of nectar, the sweet, sugary liquid they drink for energy.

Some butterflies, like the red admiral, travel from North Africa to Europe every year. No wonder they drink so much nectar!

👁 LOOK closely at a butterfly without touching it. What is it doing?

THE BODY OF A BUTTERFLY

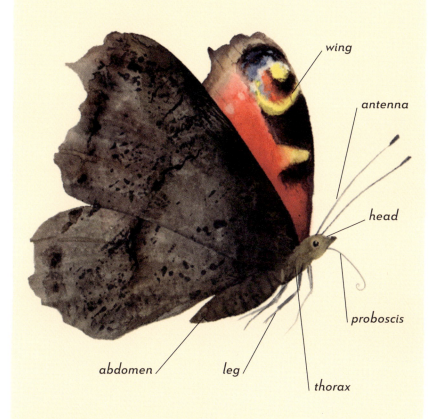

A butterfly drinks nectar from the flower through its proboscis, which is like a long straw. It uses its antennae to detect smells and wind speed, and for balance.

summer
wings

Make a hapa zome butterfly

Hapa zome is a Japanese printing technique where beautiful patterns and pictures are created by smashing leaves and flowers onto fabric. It's a fun and satisfying craft to do!

YOU WILL NEED:

- leaves and flowers
- cotton fabric (such as a piece of old bed sheet)
- a pencil or crayon
- a small hammer, mallet, or rolling pin (or a smooth, palm-sized stone)
- scissors

1. Collect some leaves and flowers. Look for different shapes and colors.

2. Fold the fabric in half and use a pencil or crayon to draw the outline of half a butterfly along the folded edge.

REMEMBER *to ask permission before picking any flowers!*

3. Unfold it again and lay it out on a hard, stable surface, like a tree stump or the pavement.

4. Arrange leaves and flowers on top of the wing you've drawn, then carefully fold the other half of the fabric over the top.

5. Take your bashing tool and gently hammer all over the fabric until you see the pattern coming through. Be careful of your fingers!

6. Unfold the fabric and remove the leaves and flowers to reveal your print.

7. Finally, cut out your fluttering butterfly!

TIP *you can also use paper instead of fabric.*

marvelous moths

What do you know about moths?

As butterflies emerge to enjoy the warmer weather, so do moths. There are a whopping 160,000 different types of moths in the world! Even though most of them are **nocturnal** and prefer to fly by the light of the moon, many varieties enjoy basking in the summer sunshine.

One mistake people often make is to imagine that moths are less lovely than butterflies. Not true! Many moths are breathtakingly beautiful, strikingly colorful, and exquisitely patterned.

Moths and butterflies have a lot in common. They even share the same life cycle. So how can you tell the difference?

There are TWO main
features that will help:

WINGS
- Moths fold their wings over their bodies in a flat, V-shape.
- Butterflies fold their wings together, pointing upward.

ANTENNAE
- Butterfly antennae are long and thin, with little nubs on the end.
- Moth antennae don't have nubs. They often look like feathery combs, and can be quite impressive!

There are a few exceptions to the rule. Some butterflies open their wings flat to "sunbathe" and a few moths close their wings upward.

summer sing-along

A poem to read at sunrise

When the heat of summer rises
and the night fades into dawn,
can you hear the birds a-calling
as you slowly stretch and yawn?

First the BLUEBIRD sings, "Good morning!"
though the sun has yet to rise . . .
Do you hear the ROBIN twitter
as you rub your sleepy eyes?

The tiny WREN will chirp
and the SLEEPY OWL will hoot . . .
It's the sound of summer music
when the CARDINAL "toot-toots!"

Chickadee sings, "summertime!"
In chickadee-dee song.
And MOURNING DOVES are cooing
in a summer sing-along!

Can you hear the WARBLERS warbling?
"Time for bed—it's getting late!"
While the trilling of the SPARROW says,
"I want to find a mate!"

At dusk the sun is setting
and the evening air is deep . . .
Now MOCKINGBIRDS are singing you
a lullaby to sleep!

A thousand lovely melodies,
each note of longing flies
until the dawn returns once more
to warm the summer skies!

These birds begin to sing roughly in the order they arrive in the poem, and most continue their songs throughout the day. The mockingbird sings both day and night.

wake up!

Listen to the dawn chorus

As the sun rises earlier in summer, so do the birds! If you wake up at daybreak, listen for the **dawn chorus**. The first birdsong begins around half an hour before sunrise, a bit like a warbling alarm clock.

Male songbirds do most of the singing. Some sing to attract a mate, while others use their voices to defend their homes and guard their chicks.

Dawn is the perfect time for SINGING. It's not yet light enough to fly out in search of food, and in the fading darkness it's much harder to be spotted by **predators**.

Dawn is the perfect time for LISTENING, when the busy noise of traffic hasn't yet begun. Birdsong carries much further when it's quiet. That's why the dawn chorus sounds so loud and clear!

Wake up before the sun rises and open your window to let birdsong trill and tumble into your ears. Or get your family up, and go for an early morning walk.

The more you listen, the more you'll hear different songs—from cheeping to chirping, chiff-chaffing to coo-cooing, tweeting, trilling, and twittering!

under shady branches

Spending time with trees

Next time you visit a green space, find the tree with the widest trunk, then reach your arms around it in a big hug! Do your fingers touch? If they do, try to find a bigger tree!

Now choose a tree with a shady canopy of leafy branches. Lie down beneath it, or sit with your back against its trunk.

On a warm summer day there is nothing as restful as being in the shade of a tree and watching dappled shadows.

 LOOK UP Can you see the sky through the leaves? How many branches can you count?

FEEL the dappled sunlight on your face. Is it cooler in the tree's shade? What does the tree's bark feel like?

 LISTEN to the wind blowing through the leaves. Do the branches groan and creak? Can you hear birdsong, or the skitter of a squirrel?

 BREATHE IN Cut grass is the scent of summer! Or maybe the ground is dry and dusty? Can you describe that smell? What words come to mind?

 LEARN The trunk of a tree continues to grow throughout its life. So trees with the widest trunks are usually the oldest. Trees can live for hundreds of years, and some even longer than that. The oldest tree in the world is almost 5,000 years old!

Can you guess how old the tree you are under is? Imagine all the things your tree has seen.

tree ID

How to identify trees by their leaves

The trees are covered in lush, green leaves in summer. Here are a few to look for:

HAZEL
- Round shape
- Pointy tip
- **Serrated** edge
- Hairy underside

ELDER
- 5 to 7 leaflets on each stem
- Oval-shaped leaflets
- Pointy tips
- Serrated edges

 LOOK What shape is the leaf? Is it shiny or dull? Are the edges rough or smooth?

📖 **LEARN** Leaves with multiple leaflets on a stalk are called **compound leaves**. A single leaf on a stalk is called a **simple leaf**.

OAK
- Wavy, rounded edges
- Narrower toward the stem
- Very short stem
- Grow in bunches

ROWAN
- 11 to 15 leaflets on each stem
- Small, thin, oval-shaped leaflets
- Serrated edges

AMERICAN CHESTNUT
- Long and thin
- Pointy tip
- Sharp-looking, serrated edges
- Up to 8 inches long

lumps and bumps

Make your own bark rubbings

Tree bark is beautiful! There are so many different patterns and textures to discover. Next time you're in the woods or a park, why not try making some bark rubbings?

YOU WILL NEED:

- crayons (remove any paper labels)
- plain paper

OPTIONAL:

- a clipboard or hardcover book
- leaves

1. Find a tree with interesting looking bark. Get up close and feel the bark with your hands. Is it rough or smooth?

2. Pick a patch of bark that you like best—perhaps it's particularly knotty, or has an unusual pattern.

👁 **LOOK** at your rubbings. What patterns do you see? Do they remind you of anything? Which is your favorite?

3. Hold a piece of paper flat against the bark and rub all over it with the side of your crayon. Press firmly to get the clearest marks and try to keep the paper as still as possible.

4. Experiment by making more rubbings from the same tree, and look for other trees with different types of bark to build up a collection!

EXTRA FUN! You can also make amazing rubbings with leaves! Place a leaf on a hard surface (such as a clipboard or book) and lay a piece of paper on top of it. Then rub your crayon over the top to reveal the leaf's pattern.

sunny days

And warm nights

In summer, Earth is tilted toward the sun. This allows the sun to shine for more hours of the day. The longer it shines, the hotter the temperature gets. When there is less wind, the weather becomes even warmer. And if it gets really hot, the heat can play tricks . . .

Standing in a field on a balmy summer day, have you noticed how the horizon seems to shimmer? Or magical puddles might appear on the pavement in the distance. This effect is called a **mirage**. It happens when heat rises from the ground and mixes with cooler air above. The more intense the heat, the more intense the mirage . . .

Stars sparkle in the night sky for a similar reason!

Nights are warmer too. On a still summer evening, the endless blue-blackness of the night sky spreads like a star-woven tapestry over our planet.

👁 **LOOK UP!** The more you stare at the stars, the more appear! If you can find a spot in the middle of nowhere, away from any **artificial light**, you might spy a shooting star . . .

Now make a wish!

📖 **LEARN** Shooting stars aren't actually stars at all, but bits of dust or rock burning up as they pass through **Earth's atmosphere**. You can still make a wish, though!

keeping time

Make your own sundial

Track the movement of the sun throughout the day by making your own simple **sundial**. You can also use it to tell time! It's best to wait for a nice sunny day to try this activity.

YOU WILL NEED:

- a long, straight stick
- 12 pebbles
- chalk or a paint pen
- a watch or phone (to tell the time)

TIP *You can start laying your pebbles at any hour of the day when there is daylight. If you miss any hours, come back the next day to complete your sundial.*

1. Pick an open, outdoor spot that will be in full sun all day.

2. Push your stick into the ground so that it stands up straight. If the ground isn't soft, you can fill a container with soil, gravel, or sand, and push your stick into the center of that instead.

👁 What direction has the shadow moved in?
Is the distance between each pebble the same?
What shape do your pebbles form?

3. Write the numbers 1 to 12 on your pebbles, using chalk or a paint pen.

4. When the clock strikes the hour, place the pebble with the number of the hour at the end of the stick's shadow.

5. Repeat the last step every hour, on the hour, until the sun sets.

TIP *You might want to set an alarm to go off a few minutes before each hour, as a reminder.*

free your feet

Going barefoot outdoors

Summer is the perfect time to take off your shoes and socks, and run barefoot through the grass!

Feeling the ground beneath your feet is one of the best ways to connect with nature—and to have fun!

Spread your toes wide and feel the solid ground on the soles of your feet. Is it rough, smooth, or stony underfoot? Does it feel warm or cold? Wet or dry?

If there is grass, does it tickle? Is it soft or prickly?

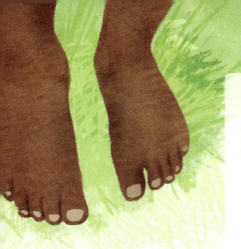

 Root your feet in the earth and pretend to be a tree swaying in the breeze.

Raise your arms overhead like branches.
Try balancing on one leg.
Can you still sway left and right?
Close your eyes and see if you can still balance.

If you ever visit the beach, how does the sand feel beneath your feet? Can you sink your toes into it?

If you like getting mucky, find a patch of dirt or mud. Pat it down with your feet until it's smooth. Can you leave a footprint?

How does playing barefoot affect your games? You will find that the more you do it, the more your feet will toughen up and the better you will feel.

cloud gazing

What can you spy in the sky?

Pack a picnic—anything will do—just some snacks and a drink. Let's spend a lazy summer day cloud gazing . . .

Find a quiet grassy spot, spread out a blanket, and enjoy your picnic. When you're ready, lie down flat on your back and stare straight up at the sky.

♡ What would it FEEL like to be a floating cloud in the sky? Imagine yourself drifting and shapeshifting.

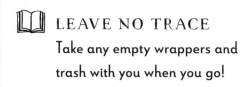

LEAVE NO TRACE
Take any empty wrappers and trash with you when you go!

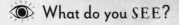 **What do you SEE?**

Clouds slowly, slowly drifting, their shapes moving, changing, and shifting . . .

Is that a great white bear huffing and puffing?

Do you see a ship sailing across the blue, blue sky?

Or is that a funny face, a hippo, a fluffy bunny . . . a dragon?

 A tiny airplane (not really tiny, just very far away) cuts through the huge blueness. It leaves a **contrail** in its wake—a trail of water droplets or ice crystals created by the jet's engine.

keeping cool

How to be cool when it's hot

On a warm summer day, it is important to drink lots of water and avoid too much sun.

Go swimming outdoors if you can, or paddle in a pond or shallow stream. Even just dipping your feet into cold water is refreshing—that's how lots of other animals keep cool in the summer.

Humans sweat when they get too hot. The water in sweat cools your skin and carries heat away from your body as it **evaporates** What do other animals do to stay cool?

Some mammals shed their winter coats and have shorter, thinner hair in summer. Some also pant- hot breath out, cool air in.

👁 **LOOK** around you! What other ways are animals keeping cool?

⭐ **BE** Imagine you are a duck gliding across a cool pond as soft, slimy weeds tickle your webbed feet!

For pigs and cows, mud is a glorious place to wallow. It forms a cooling layer of protective sunscreen on their skin.

Snakes and slow worms slide under logs and hide in damp undergrowth.

Some birds do something called "gular fluttering," where they vibrate the bones and muscles in their throat, which has a similar effect to panting.

Fish swim deeper to find shelter in the shadows.

51

treasure hunt

Searching for signs of summer

There are many treasures waiting to be found in summer. Next time you plan a trip to the park, woods, or a green space near where you live, look out for the following . . .

A BEE to hear and see. Listen to its humming. What is it doing?

Some DAISIES to pick. Can you make a chain? How many can you count?

A BIRD to listen to. Do you know what it is? Can you sing along?

A STICK to draw with. Find some dry earth and make patterns in the dust!

TIP *Summer is full of color! Why not go on a color hunt? Can you find all the colors of the rainbow in nature? A red flower, an orange butterfly, a yellow bee . . .*

A BUTTERFLY to watch. What colors are its wings?

A green, nibbled LEAF. Who's been eating it? What plant is it from?

A DANDELION to blow on. Make a wish!

A FEATHER to feel. Is it soft? What color is it?

Some BARK to touch. What does it feel like? Make a rubbing.

A perfumed FLOWER to smell. Do you know its name?

a lazy summer day

A poem to read in the shade

🖐 I FEEL the rising summer heat
from yellow grass that pricks my feet,
as off across the park we go
to find a place to take things slow . . .

☆ A dappled space beneath a tree
to read a book and just to BE
upon a warm and sunny bed
with leafy branches overhead . . .

👁 To daydream for a while and SEE
the shadow-dance of filigree,
to watch the puffing clouds pass by
like oceans rolling in the sky . . .

👃 The dusty SCENTS of summer rise—
a golden feast before my eyes,
as waving, hazy fields of grass
bewitch the insects as they pass . . .

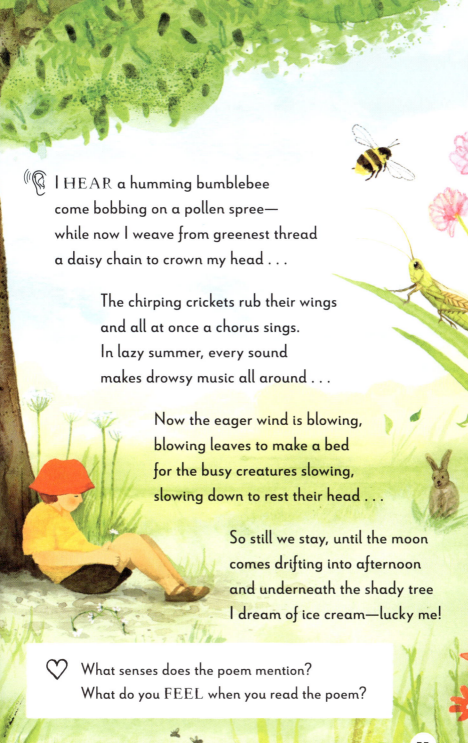

I HEAR a humming bumblebee
come bobbing on a pollen spree—
while now I weave from greenest thread
a daisy chain to crown my head . . .

    The chirping crickets rub their wings
    and all at once a chorus sings.
    In lazy summer, every sound
    makes drowsy music all around . . .

        Now the eager wind is blowing,
        blowing leaves to make a bed
        for the busy creatures slowing,
        slowing down to rest their head . . .

            So still we stay, until the moon
            comes drifting into afternoon
            and underneath the shady tree
            I dream of ice cream—lucky me!

What senses does the poem mention?
What do you FEEL when you read the poem?

be prepared

Tips for the outdoors

What to pack
Check the weather forecast before you head out to help you choose what to wear and pack.

Top tips:

- Even on sunny days, it's best to be prepared! Pack a raincoat and a warm sweater in case the weather changes.
- Even when it's hot, it's best to wear a long-sleeved top and pants to protect you from the sun and scratches.

Sweater or fleece

Raincoat

Rain boots or hiking boots

Sunscreen

Waterproof pants or overalls

Stay safe

- Never touch or pick plants without permission from an adult.
- **Foraging** for food can be fun, but don't eat anything you find outdoors unless an adult tells you it's safe.
- Make sure an adult always knows where you are and don't wander off alone.
- Be careful near ponds, rivers, and lakes. Don't go in the water without an adult nearby.

Respect wildlife

- Try to leave nature as you found it.
- Put your trash in a trash can, or take it home with you.
- Try not to disturb wild animals.

Backpack

Sun hat

Snacks

Notebook and pencil

Water bottle

field notes

Recording summer's changes

Keeping a nature journal or scrapbook is a fun and creative way to appreciate nature and track the changing seasons.

Here are some ideas to get you started:

- Draw and paint.
- Press leaves, flowers, and seeds between journal pages.
- Make rubbings—leaves, bark, and rocks work well!
- Write your own summer poems and stories.
- Keep a weather journal to track changes.
- Include photographs you've taken in nature.
  - Pick a favorite outdoor spot to return to regularly. Write down any changes that you notice between visits.
    - Make a note of the animals and plants you spot. Can you identify them all?
    - Once you've identified something, keep a tally of how many you see.

Observation notes

Here are some questions to ask yourself when you spot an animal or plant:

1. What color is it?

2. What shape and size is it?

3. What would it feel like to touch?

4. Does it have a smell?

5. What sound does it make?

summer words

artificial light
Light that is produced by sources made by humans, such as flashlights, lamps, or street lights.

chrysalis
A protective casing, or cocoon, where a caterpillar transforms into a butterfly or moth.

compound leaves
Leaves that are made up of a number of smaller leaves (leaflets) joined together on one stalk.

contrail
A white line left in the sky by the exhaust of a flying aircraft. It is made of water droplets or ice crystals produced by the aircraft's exhaust.

dawn chorus
When lots of different birds sing in the early morning.

Earth's atmosphere
The layer of gases that surrounds Earth.

evaporates
When a liquid, such as water, turns into a gas.

foraging
When a person or animal searches for food in the wild.

life cycle
A series of stages in the life of an animal or plant.

metamorphosis
When an animal changes its form as it grows, transforming into something completely different. An example of metamorphosis is a caterpillar turning into a butterfly or moth.

mirage
An optical illusion (trick of the eye) caused by hot air, which can look like a pool of water in the distance.

nectar
A sugary liquid produced by flowering plants to attract insects.

nocturnal
Nocturnal animals sleep during the day and are awake at night.

pollen
A powder produced by flowering plants to make seeds.

pollinating insects
Flying insects, such as bees and butterflies, that spread pollen between flowers.

predators
Animals that hunt and eat other animals.

serrated
Having a jagged edge, like a saw.

simple leaf
A type of leaf that consists of a single leaf on a stem.

social bees
Bees, such as honeybees and bumblebees, that live in groups.

solitary bees
Bees that live alone. Most types of bees in the world are solitary.

sundial
A device that uses the position of the sun in the sky to tell time by tracking the movement of a shadow created by a rod (known as a gnomon). Sundials are the oldest known timekeeping inventions.

index

abdomen 27
american chestnut trees 39
antennae 27, 31
ants 22

barefoot 46–47
bark rubbings 40–41, 53
bees 11, 18–19, 20–21, 52, 61
birdsong 9, 32–33, 34–35, 52
bugs 22–23
bumblebees 20
buttercups 14, 16
butterflies 9, 24–25, 26–27, 28–29, 30–31, 53

caterpillars 24–25
centipedes 23
chrysalis 24, 25, 60
clothing 56–57
clouds 9, 48–49, 54
contrail 49, 60
cool 50–51
cornflowers 13, 15
creepy-crawlies 22–23

daisies 16, 52
dandelions 13, 15, 16, 53
dawn chorus 32–33, 34–35, 60
Earth's atmosphere 43, 60
elder trees 38
evaporate 50, 60

feathers 53
field notes 58–59
flower crown 16–17
flowers 9, 10–11, 12–13, 14–15, 16–17, 18, 26, 28, 53
foraging 57, 60

grass 9
grasshoppers 22

hapa zome 28–29
hazel trees 38
honeysuckle 12, 13

insects 9, 18, 21, 22–23, 61

ladybugs 22
learn 18, 21, 37, 39, 43
leaves 9, 38–39, 53
life cycles 24–25, 60
listen 8, 34–35, 37

look 8, 22–23, 26, 36,
    38, 41, 43, 51
meadow flowers 10–11, 13, 15
metamorphosis 25, 60
millipedes 22
mirages 42, 61
moths 30–31

nectar 18–19, 26–27, 61
nights 9, 42–43

oak trees 39

petals 12, 14–15
pill bugs 22
poems 10–11, 32–33, 54–55
pollen 18, 61
poppies 13, 14
predators 34, 61
proboscis 27

rowan trees 39

safety 57
scents 9, 12, 53–54
senses 8–9, 54–55
shooting stars 43

slugs 23
smell 8, 13
snails 23
sounds 8, 32–33, 34–35,
    55, 59
stag beetles 23
stars 43
sticks 44–45, 52
sundials 44–45, 61
sunflowers 13
sunshine 42

taste 8, 13, 19
thorax 27
tips for outdoors 56–57
touch 8
treasure hunt 52–53
trees 36–37, 38–39, 40–41

wasps 21
weather 9, 42, 56
wings 27, 28–29, 31

GABBY DAWNAY

Gabby is the author of over 20 books for children, poet-in-residence at children's art and science magazine *OKIDO*, and a scriptwriter for children's television.

DORIEN BROUWERS

Dorien is an award-winning illustrator and author. She started writing and illustrating picture books as a gift for her son.

LOUISE BLACK

Louise is a Deputy Headteacher and holds a Level 3 Forest School Leader qualification. She supports providing outdoor learning for all children.